REPTILES AND AMPHIBIANS OF AFGHANISTAN

John M. Regan

This book is dedicated to the men and women who serve or have served in the Armed Forces of America. While others choose to stay at home you took a path that required courage and the vision to dramatically change your life. The great majority of Americans will never know the hazards and hardships you faced or how much they have benefited from you. In honor of you and our fallen comrades I dedicate this book.

I0121864

John M. "Jack" Regan is a retired Field Artillery officer with 23 years of active duty service. He has observed and studied wildlife around the world. Jack's articles have appeared in Reptiles Magazine and American Animal Trainer. For his volunteer work with elephants and rhinoceroses in Korea he received an award from from the mayor of Seoul, appeared on Korean television, and was featured in the Stars and Stripes newspaper. He currently lives in Washington State where he photographs and studies wildlife of the Northwest.

For more on this topic and wildlife in general visit:

Northwest Wildlife Online

Afghan Arabia Wild

The Publisher: Northwest Wildlife Online
16310 216th ST E
Graham, WA, 98338
Website: http://wwwNorthwestWildlifeOnline.com

ISBN-13: 978-0692859612 (Custom Universal)
ISBN-10: 0692859616

Other books by John M. Regan:

In a Toad's Eye (fiction)

The Commuter's Exercise Book

INTRODUCTION

From 2008 to 2011 I was team chief for a mobile training team charged with teaching operational planning to staffs of the Afghan National Army (ANA), Operations Officer for a US Army Validation Training Team, and later as Project Officer for the Afghan Army Combat Arms School. I loved my work as much as I loved my Army career but I've been a wildlife lover since the day I was born and the positions I held in Afghanistan allowed me to travel quite a bit in the country. My camera was always in hand and I took every opportunity to record every species I could. Of course, zoological expeditions in a country at war is a challenge and presents considerable limitations on one's ability to roam, especially while roaming with a large, very visible camera. For someone on active duty, security regulations and the demands of service in Afghanistan make wandering about the country side with a camera just about impossible. However, many of our forward operating bases over there are in remote locations and often positioned in or near large ANA corps areas that provide access to a surprising amount of wildlife for the alert observer. Sometimes you don't even have to look – it finds you. Like the day I swung open the door of my hootch and a snake fell on my head. It was not a venomous species and it harmlessly bounced off my head and onto my shoulder. From there it went to the ground and wriggled away. That happened a bit too quickly even for my camera finger but it does illustrate the closeness of wildlife there.

On active duty chances are good that you will run into more than one representative of Afghanistan's wildlife population.

You may not have a snake fall on your head but it could be the one that invades your billet looking for mice. Might be a gecko hiding in a Hesco, a camel spider under the piece of trash you policed up, or a hedgehog that took up residence behind a connex. Just about every service member I've ever spoken to has had one of these encounters. When you're on duty, however, you usually don't have time to get a picture of the creature and there are precious few resources to help you identify Afghan wildlife. This book is your handy pocket guide for those occasions.

Nearly every photograph in this book was taken by the author and I have provided the location of the shot. Zoo specimens or those from other sources are identified. For identification and range I relied heavily on The Reptile Data Base (Uetz, P and Jiri Hosek, editors). Dr. Uetz and his team were always a great help for reptile identification.

Table of Contents

CHAPTER ONE   ZOOLOGICAL PERSPECTIVE

It is not possible, of course, to photograph every living animal in a country the size of Afghanistan. The primary purpose of this book is first and foremost is to provide the men and women of the US military to whom this book is dedicated a quick reference guide for the kind of reptilian and amphibian wildlife they will most likely encounter in the country. Reptiles, especially serpents, tend to generate the most excitement and interest of all animals and in the arid environment of Afghanistan they definitely dominate the scene. But where you find reliably stable bodies of water a surprising number of frogs and toads pop up.

The second purpose of this book is to give any reader of it an appreciation of the amazing wildlife found in a country where the topic is scarcely, if ever, mentioned. Overshadowed by news of war, terrorism, and political chaos Afghanistan is not a country known for its wildlife. Beyond the realm of human conflict, however, lives a fascinating variety of animals in terrain that ranges from some of the highest, coldest mountains on earth to some of the hottest deserts. Afghanistan is also unique in location. The strategic location that led to its many human invaders is also responsible for its wide variety of non-human inhabitants. The frigid region of the north Central Highlands attract migrants like snow leopards, bears, and wolves that prey on spectacularly horned hoofed creatures like the markhor and Siberian Ibex. Monkeys have found a home on the central eastern border while the vast desert and semi deserts regions of the country have welcomed a range of animals very similar to many African species such as hyenas and honey badgers. Familiar European species are found here as well – badgers, otters, fox, and marmots to name a few.

Afghanistan is primarily an arid climate, however, and that is the realm of reptiles. Like dry, hot places everywhere in the world snakes and lizards rule. If you have been stationed in Afghanistan you have more than likely run into several examples of reptilian life. If you are about to get stationed there you can count on seeing your share. From the most remote regions to downtown Kabul, anywhere you go in country you'll run into snakes and lizards. In some areas you'll even be treated to a surprising number of tortoises. Don't worry about the lizards. There are no venomous species in the country. Serpents, however, are a different story. Of the nearly 40 species of serpents that inhabit the country about 8 of them are venomous, to include a viper considered to be the most dangerous snake in the world due to the number of bites it inflicts.

Amphibians are not nearly as numerous. But Afghanistan has its share of these herps and if you are anywhere near a permanent body of water be on the lookout. Despite being sadly lacking in salamanders (one single species, the Paghman Salamander) Afghanistan has large numbers of toads and even frogs. They manage to breed in even the foulest waters and spread off into the landscape in their thousands. The rare heavy rains in the south of the country causes an amusing burst of frantically feeding and breeding toads. You'll see something for sure.

CHAPTER TWO   TERRAIN

The wildlife of Afghanistan, like anywhere else in the world, is dependent on the particular terrain of the region. Afghanistan is about the size of Texas and unique in its location and the variety of its natural features. The soaring mountains north of Kabul are a startling contrast to the flat red sand desert to the south of Kandahar. The big mammals rule the north but reptiles own the largest terrain types of the country – desert, semi-desert and the steppes. There are pockets of more moist areas in the east and northeast of the country but on the whole Afghanistan is generally dry. Thanks to snow melt from the high mountain ranges and a surprising amount of underground springs, however, people and wildlife are able to survive the harsh conditions, even in the harsh summer months.

In his 2003 book "Mammals of Afghanistan", Dr. Khushal Habibi identifies 5 types of biogeographic terrain in the country:

Conifer "Monsoon" Forest

A narrow strip along the eastern border of Afghanistan affected by moisture blowing in from India this is the wettest part of the country and actually has a number of different types of forest growth.

Central Highlands

The most famous part of the country includes the Hindu Kush and the tallest mountain in Afghanistan, the Nau Shakh. Located in Badakshan the Nau Shakh is 7485 meters (about 24K feet) high. Many others are over 6000 meters. Snow melt from these mountains feed wildlife and human agriculture all the way down and beyond Kandahar. The Central Highlands are the most likely place for sightings of the biggest carnivores like wolves, bears, and Afghanistan's most famous animal – the snow leopard.

Eastern Intramontane Basin

This area lies along the eastern side of the southern slopes of the Hindu Kush Mountains out to Jalalabad where it devolves into mainly desert type terrain. This photo was taken from the Afghanistan side of the border; Pakistan is some distance beyond the mountains.

Southern Deserts

Just as fiercely hot as any Middle Eastern desert this area surrounding the Kandahar and Helmand provinces is primarily the domain of reptiles. Further south is a fascinating landscape of red sand dunes known as Registan.

Steppes

The Steppes make up a huge part of Afghanistan. Forming an enormous arc around the southern part of the Central Highlands, the steppes are known for their rugged moonscape terrain.

CHAPTER THREE   LIZARDS

Lizards in Afghanistan are not only especially plentiful they are usually quite obvious. With nearly a hundred different species inhabiting the country you are bound to see one during your time over there. Just keep your eyes open and you'll find them in the crevices of Hesco barriers in downtown Kabul, creeping about the power cables in a FOB utility shed in the middle of Lashkagar, under trash, rocks, and defunct Russian tanks, rain gutters, or clinging discreetly in the hidden corners of just about any building. In the intense heat of summer many prefer to come out at night so keep an eye out for them as the temperature cools. The desert, of course, is teaming with lizards but so are the more seasonal northeast regions. With the exception of the three foot long Indian monitor most of the lizards in the country are small, under 12 inches, and many half of that. There are no venomous species in Afghanistan and although I've caught and handled dozens I've only been bitten once. Even that was minor pinch.

Note: Since most of these species do not have a well known common name I have provided my own (in quotation marks) as well as the scientific label.

Agamids

The most abundant type of lizard in Afghanistan are the agamas. Their ubiquitous presence in the country was once recognized on an Afghan postage stamp. They are generally characterized by stout bodies and relatively large heads. Agamas prefer to hide under logs, wood piles, etc. during the day but some species are comfortable in the open. Primarily insect eaters agamas will devour about anything including vegetation, a useful adaptation for sparse environments. Many of these lizards also possess a surprising ability to change color. Although not as adept as true chameleons the color change is distinct and noticeable. Catch one and you will see this transformation in your own hand. Afghan agamas are generally no more than seven inches long and with some exceptions are unusually approachable, especially if you come near one while in a vehicle. It's as though they do not recognize it as a threat.

BRILLIANT GROUND AGAMA *Trapelus agilis*

Range: Throughout Afghanistan and the Middle East

Size: 5-6 inches

Observations: The most common variation of Agama type lizards I observed in Afghanistan are those of the *Trapelus* genus. Their accepted common name is the Brilliant Ground Agama but depending on range, breeding status, environmental conditions, and health a wide number of color variations are found. The photographs below provide an idea of just how varied in appearance this reptile is.

"PINK SPOT" *Trapelus agilis*

This guy was photographed on the grounds of Camp Lightning in Gardez in Paktika Province and was one of the first reptiles I photographed in country.

"STRIPED THROAT" *Trapelus agilis*

Photographed outside of Kandahar Airfield, this particular color pattern was the most common type I observed. They also had a very noticeable "spiny" texture to the scales on their back.

"RED BELLY" *Trapelus agilis*

This handsome specimen inhabited Camp Spann outside of Mazar-e-Shariff, Balkh Province. He had a preferred habitat alongside a fairly busy road inside the post and I could rely on his presence in mid-afternoon.

"ZEBRA-STRIPE" *Trapelus agilis*

Commonly encountered in Kandahar Province this agama displays a distinct ability to change colors when alarmed. This striped species is common throughout the country.

"BLUE THROAT" AGAMA *Trapelus agilis pakistanensis*

"Aint I pretty?" One of the more strikingly colored of the *T. agilis* species. This beautifully colored sub species of the Brilliant Ground Agama was found on FOB Lagman in Qalat, Uruzgan Province. Dozens of these small reptiles scattered out from under and old piece of plywood.

Baby *Trapelus agilis*

I would usually find a number of these little fellows in Helmand Province on the outskirts of an Afghan army brigade compound south of Lashkagar. It may have been the stark desert terrain in the area that prohibited growth or simply a coincidental discovery of baby agamas. Judging from the scale design on the lizards back it is most likely an immature "Zebra Stripe" agama.

ANDERSON'S AGAMA *Trapelus ruderatus*

Range: Throughout the Middle East; from Turkey into Pakistan
Size: Up to 12 inches long
Observations: This photo was taken in Saudi Arabia but it is a common native of Afghanistan. One notable thing about this species is its high tolerance for heat. You can see these agamas basking on rocks in the high heat of the afternoon when all other animals had disappeared to cooler hiding places. They are the largest of the agamids over there.

TOAD HEADED AGAMA *Phrynocephalus maculatus*

Range: Throughout the Saudi peninsula, north to Syria, Iran, Afghanistan, Pakistan

Size: 4 – 5 inches

Observations: The agama in the photo above ranges into Afghanistan but I took the photo in Saudi Arabia. Only five inches long it is one of the more slender, more delicate agama type lizards. The slender body type attached to the classic agama head is a key to identification.

GECKOS

The kind of lizard you are most likely to see near human habitations are the geckos. These guys are all around you in Afghanistan, some even clinging to the wall of your billet room. If not there check the surrounding buildings toward evening, especially older ones or places that are not often frequented by people. Adapted to their rocky homeland Afghan geckos rely on slender clawed toes instead of the "sticky" toes of tropical species. Generally quite small, in the range of about 5 inches, these lizards are masters at blending into their environment and are exceptionally wary in comparison to the agamids. Depending on the species they are active day or night.

ROUGH BENT-TOED GECKO *Cyrtopodion scabrum*

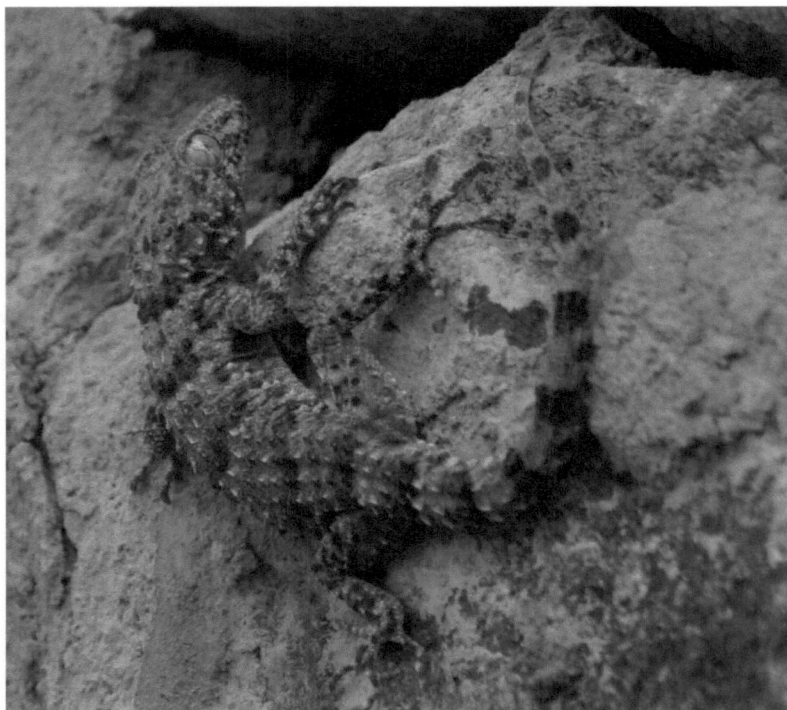

Range: Wide range from the Sudan throughout the Middle East north into Turkey and east into Afghanistan and Pakistan.

Size: 4 - 5 inches

Observations: A gecko that does not rate high on the attractiveness scale. This lizards was discovered clinging to the side of the "King's Castle" Darul Aman Palace, Kabul Province and was quite common there. They are fairly alert reptiles, however, and had to be approached cautiously in order to capture a decent photograph.

WATSON'S GECKO *Crytopodion watsoni*

Range: Throughout Afghanistan and Pakistan; likely extends further into Iran as well.

Size: 4-5 inches

Observations: One of the small Crytopodion geckos of which there are 37 known species. This specimen was photographed near Camp Dubs in Kabul Province. Both this lizard and the previously described gecko must be hibernating species as this area of Afghanistan experiences cold, often snowy winters.

CASPIAN BENT TOED GECKO *Tenuidactylus caspius*

Range: From Iran through Afghanistan and into Kazakhstan.

Size: 5 – 6 inches

Observations: Displaying the classic wide eyed gecko look these little lizards were found in two widely different areas. The lizard in the above photo made a home for itself under the wooden steps outside of my office in Camp Spann,

Mazar-e-Shariff. Its unblinking companion below, along with about a dozen others found a perfect home in a concrete utility shed on a British FOB in the middle of downtown Lashkagar, Helmand province.

BALUCH ROCK GECKO *Bunopus turberculatus*

Range: Reported range from Saudi Arabia through Iran and Afghanistan and north to Turkmenistan.

Size: 5-6 inches

Observations: Pretty in pink this beautiful little lizard is not especially common in Afghanistan. The specimen in the photo is from Saudi Arabia where I found them to be common in the desert. They are secretive lizards preferring to stay under cover during the day so there may be many more than are apparent.

Unidentified Gecko

This little gecko specimen was found clinging to the concrete wall of the "King's Castle" Darul Aman Palace. Less than two inches long the exact species has not been identified but its appearance leads me to believe it is an immature Leopard Gecko, a favorite of pet owners.

"ALLIGATOR" TYPE LIZARDS

These lizards are characterized by long, tubular bodies and long tails. They are ground dwellers often found scampering about in the open in all areas of Afghanistan. Observe areas of dried grass and vegetation closely and one of these reptiles are bound to show up.

Desert Lacerta *Mesalina guttulata*

Range: Northern Africa into Afghanistan

Size: 6 - 7 inches

Observations: Standing upright and still for a surprisingly long time the lizard in the first photo almost seemed to be posing for a portrait. Photographed on Kandahar Air Field. Also called a Small Spotted Lizard it is a common ground dwelling lizard of the region and is often found during daylight hours.

SISTAN RACERUNNER *Eremias fasciata*

Range: Middle East, Iran, Afghanistan, Pakistan

Size: 4 – 6 inches

Observations: I found these beautiful little lizards to be common in Helmand and Kandahar. Quick and quite colorful they are also energetic diggers. Often found during daylight hours. Often when hunting they will stop and vigorously wave a bright blue tail.

YELLOWTAIL FRINGE-FINGERED LIZARD *Acanthodactylus micropholis*

Range: Iran, Afghanistan, Pakistan

Size: 7 – 8 inches

Observations: Another Kandahar specimen. One of the larger and more distinctive lizards of the country, reaching lengths of 8 inches. I did not see any of these reptiles in the northern parts of Afghanistan. Mating behavior below:

BENGAL MONITOR *Varanus bengalensis*

Range: Iran, Afghanistan, Pakistan

Size: Up to 6 feet long

Observations: The above photo is from Shutter Stock I did not run into any examples of this big lizard but I have heard from several service members who had encounters with them near Jalabad in the eastern part of the country. In one of these reports the observer believes that the monitor captured and ate a cat. He did not actually see the event but the cat suddenly disappeared after the lizard arrived on the scene. Considering the size of the reptile it is very believable.

CHAPTER FOUR   SNAKES

Although not as numerous as the lizards Afghanistan has a healthy population of serpents to include several notoriously venomous species. Of the 40 or so species of serpents in the country 8 of them are considered dangerously venomous. The three most well known are described below. Others, like the Sand Racer are considered "mildly" venomous. These are rear fanged snakes that must chew a bit to inject venom but are not considered dangerous to humans, (similar to our native garter snake, a recent discovery). Despite making up a small percentage of the serpent population, however, the dangerously venomous species are the ones you are likely to encounter due to their preference for the small rodents living near human habitations. So be careful when turning over pieces of trash or rocks, etc. And keep the billets clean! There is a positive side to venomous serpents, though. Unlike harmless snakes that dash for cover, the venom producers tend to stay and fight. You get much better photographs that way! Just be careful. Afghan snakes are fairly abundant in every region of the country except the extreme north. There are no giant constrictors in the country but the Oriental Rat Snake at lengths up to nine feet will definitely get your attention should you run into one.

Saw Scaled Viper, *Echis carinatus*

Range: Very wide range from Iraq to India and north into Uzbekistan

Size: 2 – 3 feet; stout bodied

Observations: The Saw Scaled viper has earned a notorious reputation as the most dangerous snake in the world due to the number of injuries it inflicts on humans This venomous, aggressive snake is often found around human habitations due to its fondness for mice and rats. When alarmed Saw Scaled vipers rub specialized scales on their body producing a loud noise that sounds very much like "SSSHHHH!" The sound is unmistakable. Note the rather angelic design on its head and large amber eyes. This specimen along with many others was found in Kandahar. That shadow across the middle of the photo is from my left arm holding up the old pallet this snake was hiding under. The camera was in my right hand. I was pretty fortunate that day and I do not recommend this technique.

RUSSEL'S VIPER *Daboia russelii*

Range: Throughout Central and Southeast Asia

Size: 4 - 5 feet; stout bodied

Observations: Next up for dangerous notoriety is Russel's Viper. Although not as vigorously aggressive as the Saw Scaled viper this snake has an exceptionally strong strike; so strong it is reported to launch its body off the ground. The snake produces an exceptionally loud hissing sound. It has the same dietary preferences as the Saw Scale and it also attracted to human habitations but is not as common, at least in my experience. The photo above is from Shutter Stock. Based on descriptions of its behavior I believe I encountered one in a deep grassy area outside of Camp Spann in Darulaman but I was not able to get a photograph.

CENTRAL ASIAN COBRA *Naja oxiana*

Range: From Iran through Central Asia

Size: 3 – 5 feet

Observations: The king of venous snake notoriety in Afghanistan is the Central Asian Cobra. Much of this notoriety, however, is due to a now famous picture that made the rounds of the internet some time ago. In that photo one of these cobras had become stuck on a mouse glue trap. This species normally avoids humans but has a reputation for extreme aggressiveness if cornered. The serpent in the above picture is a zoo specimen; I was not able to get a photo of the one in Afghanistan.

BRAID SNAKE *Platyceps rhodorachis*

Range: Exceptionally wide range throughout the Middle East and Central Asia

Size: A very slender serpent; seldom more than 18 inches long in Afghanistan

Observations: With a bright orange stripe atop an almost lime green body this young Braid Snake was easily the prettiest serpent I found in the country. This particular specimen was discovered crawling up the wall of an abandoned building in an Afghan army training camp near Camp Spann outside of Mazar-e-Shariff. This reptile displays a variety of color patterns, however. The photo on the bottom outside of Kandahar is probably the most common pattern.

ORIENTAL RAT SNAKE *Ptyas mucosa*

Range: Enormous range from Iran to Vietnam.

Size: May exceed 9 feet

Observations: Non- venomous. After months of seeing fairly small lizards and serpents the sudden appearance of a snake almost seven feet long was quite a surprise. Easily the largest serpent in the country the Oriental Rat Snake appears to be more common in the Northern provinces where water and prey are more abundant year round. I found this specimen outside of Camp Dubs in Kabul Province. Several other sightings were relayed to me and every encounter had the same thing in common – the observer was startled by the snake's size and speed. Despite its impressive size the Oriental Rat Snake is not aggressive and normally dashes away from humans. Instead of constriction this big snake subdues prey first by biting and then sort of crushing it using its considerable body weight.

SCHOKARI SAND RACER *Psammophis schokari*

Range: Widespread throughout North Africa and into Afghanistan and Pakistan

Size: Slender bodied, about 2 feet in length as adults

Observations: Rear fanged; mildly venomous. A common species in the country and the Middle East but rather difficult to catch or photograph due to the extraordinary quickness of the serpent. This specimen was captured in Saudi Arabia.

SPOTTED WHIPSNAKE *Hemorrhios ravergieri*

Range: Central Asia from Turkey to Mongolia

Size: 4 – 5 feet

Observations: Non-venomous. Although color variations occur the speckled appearance of the snake is obvious in the photographs. This specimen was found outside of Camp Dubs in Kandahar Province rapidly trying to escape the gate guard attempting to kill it.

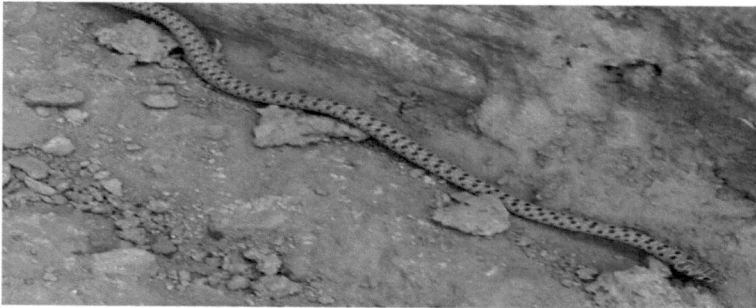

DERAFSHI SNAKE *Lytorhynchus ridgewayi*

Range: Throughout Iran and east into Afghanistan and Pakistan; north to Uzbekistan

Size: No data

Observations: This unfortunate serpent got stuck in a glue trap and was brought to my office in the Afghan National Army Training Education Center. I managed to free it from the trap but the poor thing did not survive the operation. It is the only example of the species I observed.

CHAPTER FIVE – TOROISES

This is a very short chapter because there is only one known member of the Testudinas (turtle) family in Afghanistan. While the overall climate is favorable to reptiles in general this does not apply to aquatic turtles which require an abundance of water. The land dwelling tortoises are also not as common as their aquatic cousins in most of their range. The Audubon Society Field Guide to Reptiles and Amphibians identifies 60 aquatic turtles but just three tortoises in North America for example, and only 39 different species worldwide. A likely reason for this is that a slow moving animal in a dry climate has a much more difficult time finding food. Afghan tortoises appear to be very common in the central to southern provinces, an observation gleaned from conversations with a number of soldiers.

AFGHAN TORTOISE *Testudo horsfieldii*

Range: Iran through Central Asia and into south Russia and China according to some references

Size: Fairly large member of the turtle family; carapace about 12 inches long

Observations: This pair was lovingly cared for by soldiers in a small FOB outside of Qalat in Zabul Province. Often sold in pet shops as a Russian Tortoise this member of the turtle family is surprisingly common in some parts of Afghanistan.

Chapter SIX – AMPHIBIANS

Known for its arid climate, Afghanistan is not a particularly welcome habitat for amphibians, and there certainly are a lot more reptiles hanging around. The country is home, however, to several interesting species of frogs and toads. To date there is just one species of salamander identified - the Paghman Salamander, found in the Paghman Mountains north of Kabul. This salamander is an unlikely find for anyone but a dedicated searcher. Frogs and toads, however, are likely finds, some in quite unexpected locations or thriving in water so polluted you'd think nothing could survive in it.

The above photos were taken outside of Camp Dubs and are most likely tadpoles and immature species of Green Toads. The pair of empty plastic bottles in the picture does not relay the true state of oily pollution and garbage in this stream that ran alongside an Afghan army motor pool.

GREEN TOAD *Pseudepidalea viridis*

Range: From Europe through central Asia into Russia

Size: Up to 5 inches long

Observations: A common toad found throughout Afghanistan and all the other "Stans," Like a number of species of Afghan wildlife it is also a very common in Europe. The brownish specimen in the above photo was found on Kandahar Airfield. The other little guy was discovered hopping around right inside the concrete walls of Camp Dubs.

IRANIAN TOAD *Bufo surdus*

Range: Iraq to Pakistan

Size: 2-3 inches from nose to tail.

Observations: A very common inhabitant it also bears the common name of the Iranian Earless Toad. They range from Iran into Pakistan and were found in large numbers in Kandahar around anyplace with consistent water but spend the day tucked away under rocks, logs, or any available cover.

The photos on the following page have also been identified as an Iranian Toad. But this very small, less than 2 inches, stout bodied toad was found in great numbers in watery areas near on the Kandahar Air Field. Also very smooth skinned. Possibly an immature Iranian Toad.

Iranian Toad – more photos

SKITTERING FROG *Euphlyctis cyanophlyctis*

Range: Central and South Asia

Size: 3 -4 inches

SKITTERING FROG *Euphlyctis cyanophlyctis*

Observations: A large number of these interesting frogs were found in a small reservoir on the Kandahar Airfield. From a floating position in the water Skittering Frogs bounce across the surface when alarmed instead of diving for cover like most frogs. It is a real treat to witness 20 or 30 of these small frogs suddenly splatter the surface of a pond in all directions. Of all the animals I photographed in Afghanistan none has attracted as much attention as the skittering frog.

EXTENDED SPECIES LIST

Reptiles:

The Reptile Data Base **(Uetz, P and Jiri Hosek, editors)**

http://www.reptile-database.org/

SQUAMATA – LIZARDS

Eremias grammica (LICHTENSTEIN, 1823)

Eremias lineolata (NIKOLSKY, 1897)

Eremias nigrocellata NIKOLSKY, 1896

Eremias persica BLANFORD, 1875

Eremias regeli NIKOLSKY, 1905

Eremias scripta (STRAUCH, 1867)

Eremias velox (PALLAS, 1771)

Eryx elegans (GRAY, 1849)

Eublepharis macularius (BLYTH, 1854)

Eumeces blythianus (ANDERSON, 1871)

Eumeces schneideri (DAUDIN, 1802)

Eurylepis taeniolata BLYTH, 1854

Eutropis dissimilis (HALLOWELL, 1857)

Hemidactylus flaviviridis RÜPPELL, 1835

Laudakia agrorensis (STOLICZKA, 1872)

Laudakia melanura BLYTH, 1854

Laudakia nupta (DE FILIPPI, 1843)

Laudakia nuristanica (ANDERSON & LEVITON, 1969)

Laudakia tuberculata (GRAY, 1827)

Mesalina guttulata (LICHTENSTEIN, 1823)

Mesalina watsonana (STOLICZKA, 1872)

Ophiomorus brevipes (BLANFORD, 1874)

Ophiomorus chernovi ANDERSON & LEVITON, 1966

Ophiomorus raithmai ANDERSON & LEVITON, 1966

Ophiomorus tridactylus (BLYTH, 1853)

Ophisops jerdonii BLYTH, 1853

Paralaudakia badakhshana (ANDERSON & LEVITON, 1969)

Paralaudakia caucasia (EICHWALD, 1831)

Paralaudakia erythrogaster (NIKOLSKY, 1896)

Paralaudakia himalayana (STEINDACHNER, 1867)

Paralaudakia lehmanni (NIKOLSKY, 1896)

Paralaudakia microlepis (BLANFORD, 1874)

Phrynocephalus clarkorum ANDERSON & LEVITON, 1967

Phrynocephalus euptilopus ALCOCK & FINN, 1897

Phrynocephalus interscapularis LICHTENSTEIN, 1856

Phrynocephalus luteoguttatus BOULENGER, 1887

Phrynocephalus maculatus ANDERSON, 1872

Phrynocephalus mystaceus (PALLAS, 1776)

Phrynocephalus ornatus BOULENGER, 1887

Phrynocephalus raddei BOETTGER, 1888

Phrynocephalus reticulatus EICHWALD, 1831

Phrynocephalus scutellatus (OLIVIER, 1807)

Pseudopus apodus (PALLAS, 1775)

Ptyas mucosa (LINNAEUS, 1758)

Ptyas nigromarginata (BLYTH, 1854)

Saara asmussi (STRAUCH, 1863)

Saara hardwickii (GRAY, 1827)

Tenuidactylus caspius (EICHWALD, 1831)

Tenuidactylus fedtschenkoi (STRAUCH, 1887)

Tenuidactylus longipes (NIKOLSKY, 1896)

Tenuidactylus turcmenicus (SZCZERBAK, 1978)

Tenuidactylus voraginosus (LEVITON & ANDERSON, 1984)

Teratoscincus bedriagai NIKOLSKY, 1900

Teratoscincus keyserlingii STRAUCH, 1863

Teratoscincus microlepis NIKOLSKY, 1900

Teratoscincus scincus (SCHLEGEL, 1858)

Trachylepis septemtaeniata (REUSS, 1834)

Trapelus agilis (OLIVIER, 1807)

Trapelus megalonyx GÜNTHER, 1864

Trapelus ruderatus (OLIVIER, 1804)

Trapelus sanguinolentus (PALLAS, 1814)

Varanus bengalensis (DAUDIN, 1802)

Varanus griseus (DAUDIN, 1803)

Xenochrophis piscator (SCHNEIDER, 1799)

SQUAMATA SERPENTES - SNAKES

Boiga trigonata (SCHNEIDER, 1802)

Bungarus caeruleus (SCHNEIDER, 1801)

Echis carinatus (SCHNEIDER, 1801)

Eirenis persicus (ANDERSON, 1872)

Elaphe dione (PALLAS, 1773)

Eristicophis macmahoni ALCOCK & FINN, 1897

Eryx elegans (GRAY, 1849)

Eryx johnii (RUSSELL, 1801)

Eryx miliaris (PALLAS, 1773)

Eryx tataricus (LICHTENSTEIN, 1823)

Gloydius halys (PALLAS, 1776)

Hemorrhois ravergieri (MÉNÉTRIES, 1832)

Liopeltis frenatus (GÜNTHER, 1858)

Lycodon striatus (SHAW, 1802)

Lytorhynchus maynardi ALCOCK & FINN, 1897

Lytorhynchus ridgewayi BOULENGER, 1887

Macrovipera lebetina (LINNAEUS, 1758)

Myriopholis blanfordi (BOULENGER, 1890)

Myriopholis longicauda (PETERS, 1854)

Naja naja (LINNAEUS, 1758)

Naja oxiana (EICHWALD, 1831)

Natrix tessellata (LAURENTI, 1768)

Oligodon arenarius VASSILIEVA, 2015

Oligodon taeniolatus (JERDON, 1853)

Platyceps karelini (BRANDT, 1838)

Platyceps ladacensis (ANDERSON, 1871)

Platyceps rhodorachis (JAN, 1865)

Platyceps ventromaculatus (GRAY, 1834)

Psammophis leithii GÜNTHER, 1869

Psammophis lineolatus (BRANDT, 1838)

Psammophis schokari (FORSKAL, 1775)

Pseudocerastes persicus (DUMÉRIL, BIBRON & DUMÉRIL, 1854)

Ptyas mucosa (LINNAEUS, 1758)

Ptyas nigromarginata (BLYTH, 1854)

Spalerosophis diadema (SCHLEGEL, 1837)

Telescopus rhinopoma (BLANFORD, 1874)

Xenochrophis piscator (SCHNEIDER, 1799)

TESTUDINES - TURTLES

Testudo graeca (LINNAEUS, 1758)

Testudo horsfieldii (GRAY, 1844)

AMPHIBIAN SPECIES LIST from
"CONSERVATION BIOLOGY OF AMPHIBIANS OF ASIA"

ANURA – FROGS AND TOADS

Bufotes oblongus (Nikolski 1896)

Bulfotes pewzowi (Bedriaga 1898)

Bufotes psuedoraddei (Mertens 1971)

Bufotes turanensis (Hemmer, Schmidtler, and Bohme, 1976)

Dutraphrynus olivaceus (Blandford, 1874)

Dutraphrynus stomaticus (Lutken, 1865)

Chrysopaa sternosignata (Murray, 1885)

Euphlyctis cyanophlyctis (Schneider, 1799)

Hoplobatrachus tigerinus (Daudin, 1802)

Pelophylax ridibundus (Pallas, 1771)

CAUDATA - SALAMANDERS

Paradactylodon musterci (Smith, 1940)

REFERENCES:

ONLINE:

The Reptile Data Base (Uetz, P and Jiri Hosek, editors)

http://www.reptile-database.org/

Little Scorpion – website by Mike Arthur

http://littlescorpion.com

iNaturalist. Org - website devoted to wildlife around the world

http://iNaturalist.org

Wikipedia – well known, immensely useful website

Afghan Arabia Wild – website of the author

Northwest Wildlife Online – website of the author

HARD COPY:

Habibi, K., 2003. Mammals of Afghanistan

Cogger, Harold G. and Zweifel, Richard G., 2003. Encyclopedia of Reptiles and Amphibians

Heatwole, H. and Das, I., 2014. Conservation Biology of AMPHIBIANS OF ASIA

US Army Center for Health Promotion and Preventive Medicine poster – "Venomous Snakes of Southwest Asia"

Behler, J. and King, F., 2013, National Audubon Society Field Guide to Reptiles and Amphibians

2010 Map
From Stars and Stripes

www.ingramcontent.com/pod-product-compliance
Lightning Source LLC
Chambersburg PA
CBHW041225270326
41934CB00001B/1